# BareBackMagazine

January 2014

This is a work of fiction. The characters, incidents, and dialogue are the products of the authors' imaginations and are not to be construed as real. Any resemblance to actual events or person, living or dead, is entirely coincidental.

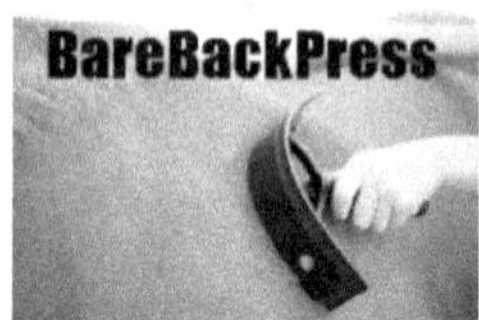


BareBackPress
Hamilton, Ontario, Canada
For enquires visit www.barebackpress.com
For information contact press@barebacklit.com

Editors Peter Jelen and Damon Ferrell Marbut
Cover layout and art: "Some Kid the Artist Saw Somehow Managing to Talk on a Cell Phone While at the Same Time Listening to an iPod" © Peter Jelen.


ISBN-13: 978-0992035532
ISBN-10: 0992035538

## POETRY



## FICTION



## FLASH FICTION

## FEATURED POET
## Carl Miller Daniels



## THOUGHT

# POETRY

# The Meat Rack
## Brian Strauss

High top sneakers squealing on the feet of a queer walking by
thunderously crashing to the ground with each step. Strange-
like gracefulness to the stride though, almost floating
above the crash of the rubber to the pavement.

Some spick, dancin' in the moonlight
thinks he's real hot-shit the way
he moves his feet, really shuffles those fuckers,
glaring up at me with a flirtatious snark.

Light a cigarette; watch the smoke trail off like a
blinding rail of light reflecting against the droplets of sunshine
that hadn't completely washed away from the sky
as the moon perched itself high above the edge of reason.

Slide my hand across the table, gently over hers
and feel that warmth emanating, a hot coal in my grasp.
Give her the chance to pull back, then hard and firm,
remember you're a man. Act accordingly.

Look at the way she fiddles with her hair,
the way she chews her nails, and looks at her feet.
Take notice of her nervously biting the corner of her lip,
tender pink pillows, luscious and moist.

That little spick's still there swayin' his hips
like pendulums of flesh swinging
to some unheard pulse, some soundless rhythm.
Keep your eye on the girl, lean in close.

Don't jump the gun though. Pull back and light another
cigarette, make her really want it, let her build it up
in her own mind. You won't disappoint, you know that.
You're just... looking for a bit of attention.

**About the Author:**
Brian Strauss is a poet interested in exploring the boundaries of language and the possibilities of emotional spatiality. Within these interests he strives to entertain and challenge traditional notions of morality and identity through the facets of sound and structural experimentation. For poetry and music by Brian Strauss please visit *www.facebook.com/defband*

## Romusico
## David L. Butler

The piano will twinkle with the eyes,
The guitar will give form to the shape,
The bass will give the strength to stand,
The drum will hold the body straight,
And with confidence in the sound,
Rhythm within the beat of the step,
Romeo will emerge from the shadows,
Looking up to sing her down,
For this scene is not complete,
Without his Juliet.

**About the Author:**
David L Butler is a writer, filmmaker and film editor, and has an interest in the arts in general. Although he has not had any professional success, he has been writing for over 20 years – lyrics, stories, stage plays and film scripts - and is a three time nominated and one time award winning filmmaker.

## Divination
## Martina Reisz Newberry

It's late autumn
and I am here
to read your palm.

You will not die young.
You will not become
a celebrity.

You will never be rich,
only somewhat "well off."
It won't be enough.

You will be as I am—
a fool without breath
to blow away the unrealities.

Don't despair.
Everything gives way
to something else

and no one is strong enough
to hold on to music
or the moon.

You are no exception.
Think. What is there
that can be imprisoned in a book?

A child holding
a mangled doll by its arm
is no more solvent,

matters no more
than the outside lights
with no place to go

except into your window.
Never ask yourself
if winter is here,

can spring be far behind?
Hell yes, it can.
It can be centuries,

eons, millenniums behind.

Your deliquescence
is a different story.

It is at hand,
dissociated, alien,
unremembered.

Forgive me,
this is all your
palm says.

**About the Author:**
Martina Reisz Newberry's most recent book is LEARNING BY ROTE (Deerbrook Press). She is also the author of seven collection of poems. Her poetry has appeared in numerous journals over the past four decades. A new book, WHERE IT GOES, is forthcoming in 2014 from Deerbrook Editions.

# Mal's Petal World
## Jane Brooke

White girl, white hair, white skin, white tears, cut and faceted lapis colored eyes, lazing naked in a bed of white flowers, soaring stems of the petal world, capricious moods, prayer and quiet, silent cries to the timorous sky and mending her fatigue in a moment of disquietude, as morning breeze, summer char, a saffron fireball, sizzling tinge, thermal winds, a shawl of summer sweetness plies along her alabaster skin.

I am sitting near the monarchs home, near the circle of the Monet colored spun spider webs, filled with dew drops that glisten from shards of Sun and remnant rainbows of the rains, of winter they have fled, though moments ago as faceted tourmaline's they were dancing powdered wings along her face, her Amber eyes, a face that I so do adore. I am gazing at her as I always do and I am afraid to wake her, for what if she does not want me any longer when her eyes of a topaz Sun, might perhaps peek open as the color of cinnamon, and within that moment she no longer loves me, sees suddenly she sees the charlatan that was once me and once again I will become the jesters fool.

I am watching her, I always watch her when she sleeps, and I remember what and who I was before her, before she brought jasmine, incense, diamonds and happiness to my dreams, as a gift few women, few fools as I have ever seen.

I think back as an echo that repeats itself within a long lost moment of memory that I shudder to recall, for I was only part human before her, pretending to be alive, not living, no not at all, as if some ancient star long lost and dead in the blackness of the stratosphere, that now only glimmers its last tear, as it breaks earth's gravity, a thief of fractured dreams, a piece of light, masquerading to be alive as I was before her, as a fragile flickering flame of candle light. I was human, yet disposable, a lost girl barely breathing before she choose to delve within my mind and only me, before she shared her gift of smile, genius, mirth and wit for each and every other human being to see.

I am in pain as memory sears my mind, for I was a mimic of a girl, shattered, fractured and refracted in a liquid mercury pool of skin, as images, none true, none real, remind me of a lying past and such a horrid way and forever and all of my so banal and carnal sins. There was a desert in my heart, until she looked into my soul and forgave me for who I was and what I was so long ago and when, knowing that her elegance and intelligence and great heart would repair the broken mirror that I had always been.

I am watching her, I always watch her as she sleeps and when she wakes, I will have cut flowers for her and they will be white like her, delicate and elegant, children of the soil that I gathered near the lakes. She and them, her and they, they are sisters of the petal world and will make her smile and she will touch my face and kiss my lips and I can ask for nothing more, for the flowers, so like her, so fragile and powerful and lovely are the color of the scattered matrix of the rainbow world. With in a moment of a slivered moon, bathed within a golden glow and the warmth of down, the cold of snow and we will whisper as we touch each other's lips, that neither bigotry, pain or sadness will ever be a part of our lives again. Naked women, white sheets, passion and a tender touch of whispers within the grey pewter morning dawn and I will tell her that I love her so, and the Monarch Butterflies, winged wind whisperers will lead us home, through the wars and battle fields of a life neither of could ever understand and thus, our lives will soar and the gift of her will be mine as long as she deems it so, I can ask for nothing else, for one can never grasp and keep forever the beauty of a rainbow, this I clearly know.

**About the Author:**

Jane Brooke, is a 22 year old stick blond savage lesbian London writer of mostly LGBT fiction. In 2013 she has 9 new novels out at Amazon Books, and a heathen, she would, like DeSade, write with her on blood on a prison wall, if chained to a cot,, if that was the only venue open for to her to write. You can see her page at Facebook, Jane Brooke. If you would like to chastise her for her work, you can at *janebrookeerotica@yahoo.com*

## Cockamamie
## Michael Estabrook

My sublimation technique is working fine
Whenever the slightest sexual urge or image
arises to tempt me
whenever I catch a glimpse of the pure white
of her inner thigh or notice her
tucking her hair behind an ear
or get distracted by the gleam
of her pink passion toenail polish
or the tightness of her blouse
I immediately redirect my focus
and begin reciting the books
of the Old Testament
or Shakespeare's plays in order
of composition and first performance

Yes Freud would be proud of me I think
adhering so well to his theories for detouring
my useless libidinal impulses
into enhanced artistic creativity

Or he might shake his head instead
tell me what an idiot I am
for paying attention to his cockamamie ideas
and say go ahead and fuck her
you moron

**About the Author:**
After 40 years working for "The Man" and "The Woman" Michael Estabrook is finally free. No more useless meetings in stuffy windowless rooms. He can concentrate instead on making better poems and on other interests: history, art, theatre, and his wife who remains the most beautiful woman he has ever known

## We are the other parents
## Rob Thomas

The mom is apoplectic.
"How could you do this to me?" she thunders.

You'd think the kid had shit in her pants
rather than his own.

"You don't deserve to be at the park,"
she rages.

And the kid knows enough to cower.
We grimace and avoid eye contact.

We are the other parents
for a change.

**About the Author**:
Rob Thomas lives in Ottawa. He won the 2013 *John Newlove Poetry Award* and is working on his first chapbook. It will be launched at the Ottawa International Writer's Festival. He has three young children and has successfully toilet trained dozens of poems. *www.robthomas.ca*

# Brief Observations of Things in the Margin

## Ali Znaidi

Foam on the pavement.
—The spittle of a drained
prostitute.

***

Call me whatever!
But I won't change my position
in the dark.

***

Instead of committing suicide
useless water perishes in
the sewers.

**About the Author:**
Ali Znaidi (b.1977) lives in Redeyef, Tunisia where he teaches English. His work has appeared in *Stride Magazine*, *Red Fez*, *BlazeVox, Otoliths, streetcake, Ygdrasil,* & elsewhere. His debut poetry chapbook Experimental Ruminations was published in September 2012 by *Fowlpox Press* (Canada). From time to time he blogs at *aliznaidi.blogspot.com.*

# Exhibit: Tombstone
## Sarah Nguyen

Standing quiet and tall
The clean lines cut through the silence of the room.

Smooth, cold marble
Sending chills as you approach

Reflecting on its purpose
Strength and love resonate beyond the hardness of its walls.

Shadows of its life
Dancing gracefully across the velvet surface

Scarred with intent
Retreating in the comfort of its hollow curves.

Gazing until you realize
The beauty of a legacy left

Honor and loyalty
Engraved into the stone and in my mind.

A monument of truth and reality
Boasting under bright track lighting

Preserving a history
To live on in all that walk by.

Please do not touch.

**About the Author:**
Minneapolis native Sarah Nguyen is currently studying design and exploring outlets in creativity (such as taking poetry writing class). Sarah's pursuit of design and travel gives her a profound perspective on her surroundings and can be seen in her everyday life happening.

# I write poetry
## Nicolas Fleurot

I write poetry
Because I am financially suicidal
I write poetry
Like thousands of others
Poets who try to sell me their books I can't buy because I wasn't able to sell my own

I write poetry
Because I see fluffy colours
I see ashes dancing in the rain
I write poetry
Because I see Light in the shape of a horse galloping in the shadow of your Love

I write poetry
Because I didn't have the right balls or the right drugs to become a rock star

I write poetry
Because sometimes at night I hug the darkness and the stars become diamonds and the dust become gold and dreams become butterflies that never die

I write poetry
Because I talk to teddy bears

I write poetry
Because that is what I see in people

I write poetry
Because that is what I did most of my Life

I write poetry.

**About the Author:**
Nicolas Fleurot is a French poet and artist born in 1980. Since 2000, his poems have been published in several poetry magazines and anthologies. Fleurot resides now in Ireland and works and writes in English. He also appears as an extra in various short / feature movies. He likes robots, zombies and thinks that when the sea reflects the sky, the birds drink clouds. www.facebook.com/nicolasfleurot

## Everything Changes
## T.J. Cheverie

There's a certain point, when day turns to night
When reality turns into dreams
And where the truth reveals itself for all to see
Everything changes if given enough time
Even people, whether we choose to recognize it or not
Though the sky in the East in dark and gloomy
The sky in the West and bright and promising
Humanity lives beneath two great prophets of ancient origins
The sun always follows the moon, and the moon always follows the sun
I watch them both pass by from my windowsill
Do you ever reminisce about the ones you've lost who you loved?
We never appreciate what we have until we lose it
Before a mountain rises from the sea, no one knows it's a mountain
I see polar shifts every day when I go to the market places
People fall only to rise again in some form or another
So today, rise up and embrace your metamorphosis
For tomorrow, everything will change forever, including you.

**About the Author:**
T.J. Cheverie is a Canadian artist in Pemberton, British Columbia. T.J. won the 2012 Mayor's Poetry Challenge in Whistler for his poem Time, and was published in Garbanzo Literary Journal for his poem Binary Love Code . Currently, he is hard at work dreaming and contributing daily to the human story.

# FICTION

# In a Dry Season
## Jim Finley

I know what a dry season is. And I know what it ain't. It mostly throw-down trotline luck. And I ain't cut bait since the last rain. It only take a crooked grin to piss on my fire right now. With luck so stingy I ain't expecting no trophy. Just cruising, running the line, chasing my habit. Yesterday morning I stop at a light and just that quick the earth shifts. The sun come out. The blue bird sing. Luck come rapping on my door. Like I say, I spot one walking out a free clinic. She look ripe, so I tail to know where she stay. It my policy to scope-out one day, pay regard the next. When I see her car, it come to me that I done got the deed on this one. I tail her Christmas last. She cut her lights and slipped down a back street. Oh yes, mama, I take my hat off to you. But the meter running now, bitch. You're on my time. Fact is, your final marker done been etched and dated. About then my groin go tight and a tic jump on my face. It the same ever time.

She must stay fifteen mile outside of town, but I count her worth it. I know she seen me. Just like before. She a spunky bitch. White knuckle gripping the wheel, speeding back streets, then kicking it full-tilt out on the asphalt. Her eye glued to the rear-view from the git-go. I stop down from her house and stake-out til after dark. Don't see nothing. Not even a kitchen light.

I get home early, but can't catch no sleep. Next morning my heart do thc boogla-loo, but it my policy to wait late afternoon to pay regard. Let the muscle of the new day gather slack. Disengage. Unwind. Go drowsy. Thinking on that throw a spring in my step. I crave a nerve brew, so I snare a Jack Daniel and float through the early day.

Later I park side the highway and come up her slope eyeballing a sun sinking behind the slant roof, pitching shadow down to the road. A devil-duster kick up atop the rise and twist down toward the ditch. It carry a smell of desperation, a sour smell that leave a trace of bitterness, a hefty hint of rot and ruin. Suddenly a bolt of fear rip through me, taking a bite of both legs. My mind jack-up bout poor whitey, bout rednecks being leather-tough and junk-dog mean.

The house stand off the ditch and up a lazy rise. Everthing dead. The land grow nothing but pipeline running ever whichaway. Just baked dirt, dirt so hard it shine. Dead mesquite and wire-weed climb the slope. Tumbleweed break loose and blow agin the house. A cur bitch slink from neath the porch and drop to the ground. Her tongue hang in the dirt. Boards missing off the house. The paint been powdered and eat off by sandstorms. Just as well. Nothing hold paint in Stonewall County. A window been boarded up with rotted crisscross one-bys. The front door near bout gone. It just slack screen hanging crooked.

After a minute or so I top the rise and that when I seen her. It catch me up short and slap me flat-faced. I swear I go monkey-eyed. After all, such sight don't put my sort in no temper for pitching washer or gigging frog. It the bitch all right! Cept now she showing bare tit with a baldhead naked baby riding her hip. She appear sudden out the dark behind the screen. I plant my eye on what before me, standing there in almighty glory, her perky tits saluting the flag. No ounce of fear on her face. I swear I couldn't ask God for more. I draw up in a ball of hard flesh and pigeons commence fluttering and flapping in the bottom of my belly. My skin start to move and fore long I'm itching to bump up agin something, something soft but firm.

Ain't seen such a sugar-sweet sight in all my twenty-two year. I knew she were fine, but I could never dream such as this. Her hair, sun-baked and frilly, put a light in her blond eyes. I edge closer while she bounce the baby to the other hip. Her upside jiggle and again set me to burning. A hot flash jolt my body once, then twice more. Meanwhile her baby grab a nipple. I'm close now, walking fast, cutting the distance, my mind going numb. Suddenly, I catch a scent and it smell like collard green on to cook. A grasshopper take wing with a singing whine as I two-step the rickety porch. She don't move cept to turn and put the baby on the floor. She then come up slow, but straight as a young pine to front me. She don't scream. She don't smile. She don't say hello. She just push open the screen and I step on the inside.

Without no window it mostly dark there in the room. I hold what I got to let my eye settle. Right away I smell sour sweat and whiskey. He in a far corner sitting a straight-back chair. He sitting upright and stiff, dragging on a short fag. His face but a boney shadow in the glow of the cigarette. A two-barrel scattergun rest easy cross his leg. I take in a deep breath.

It over now. I should know better. It had to catch me up sometime. Ain't nothing free in this world. Not one fucking thing.

**About the Author:**
Most fiction Jim Finley writes is grounded in the place and spirit of his youth; in the shadows of the Brazos Salt Fork, near 6666 Ranch, somewhere south of sorrow and north of nothingness. Youth for him was the 1950s, but even today, this single slice of Texas and the people it marks remain sacred.

# Trip of a Lifetime
## Carolyn V. Egan

That digital billboard with the damn parakeet squawking about something or other. What was it? Oh yeah. The dream of a lifetime. Where was I? Let me think. I was leaping down, three steps at a time, down to the subway to catch the last train out - to where? Let me think. I was running out of time. The plumes of ghastly atmosphere, you know what I mean. That rotten cloud of excrement and sweat and who knows what putrid crap that greets you, smothers you really…as you enter that underground charnel pit with the turnstiles clanging behind you making you feel like you won't ever get out. It's a one-way trip. That's what I smelled or smelled me. That's where I was going.

Anyway that damn parakeet was croaking in 3-D about a dream of a lifetime. Or a trip of a lifetime. Or was it a lifetime of a trip?

That was my life, a real trip. My mother called it heron, like a bird. In her time, anyway, it was a bird that danced over their nodding heads, clawing to get to their brains. But the brains were too low in their skulls, almost in their throats, hiding really.

I think my brain was somewhere else too, lurking. In my knuckles, maybe, because my fists had a mind of their own. They'd bunch up and squeeze into hard little stones and roll around in my pockets and then jump out like rockets and flail and jab when I needed them to, punching whatever was in my way. Yeah, they knew what they were doing and I'd follow them around, hoping they had a plan.

I needed a fix. Ooh. That's it. I was sick with it. Real sick. I was doubled over, feeling like I might have to hurl - waiting for my train. Where was I going? That cement platform was all shiny with urine and puke and bits from people's pockets stuck to it like little shivering flags. And that jabbering parakeet, as big as a person, was over my head, over the heads of all the nodding bums huddled against the splattered walls with their fists deep in their pockets and their eyes shut in tight grimaces, like they were under that parakeet's spell. A trip of lifetime. Get your ticket here.

I was standing there under that giant bird, waiting for my train, the winds of the southbound tunnel sweeping me in like a toilet flush.

That's when something from my 9th grade science class came to me. Something about all the atoms of every solid thing being surrounded by space. It occurred to me then, in that minute, that nothing was connected really. Around everything was space. Even in this underground hole - just outer space, nothing solid. So that damn parakeet could fly off the billboard and start clawing at my brain cause there was nothing really holding that green bird to the wall.

My fists started leaping and quivering in my pockets, when the brain in them got it. Got that the parakeet was like today's heron, getting ready to rip at brains.

Oh man. I needed a fix bad.

When I turned to face that billboard with that monster ready to fly at me, I saw this lady next to me in green tall shoes, like stilts, a pointy yellow party hat and long red carving nails. She wasn't moving, not a stitch. Staring straight ahead like one of those fashion dolls in store windows.

"Hey," I said, because I needed conversation.

"Lady, what's the time?"

Her head turned like it could go all the way around and look backwards. Then it stopped and she blinked flat eyes at me. She pursed her mouth like she was going to blow me a kiss.

"Time to feed the parakeet," she screeched as my train swept in, with that infernal scream of metal breaking. And my spine was on fire and my head was split open and my trembling fists were jerking in my pockets for cover.

And the last thought I had was:

This is a trip of a damned lifetime.

**About the Author:**

Carolyn V. Egan has been an instructor of writing and English at multiple colleges and institutions since 2000. Among other academic writing awards, she has won the Connecticut College Fiction Prize. She has been published in *Newsweek* and *Angels on Earth* magazines and subsequently anthologized in the high school textbook, *Expository Composition, Discovering Your Voice*. I have a BA in English from Connecticut College and a JD from the University of Connecticut, School of Law. Learn more on *www.pastiche.name* and follow her at *twitter.com/Nagevc*.

# Jacob
## Alyssa Crowder

He strode into the coffee shoppe with the sort of heel-toe confidence and ease that every young man his age wishes for. Clad from his broad shoulders to his long and slender feet in a mix of black and gray, he settled into the line to order his usual café mocha. Jacob seldom ever had to question neither himself nor his appearance. His smoldering brown eyes were warm and sensitive the very way a loving parent's would be. He was well aware of his edged face complete with a hard jawline, and his perfectly sculpted slender rose colored lips. His nose was long and poised in the very middle of his face, making him very aesthetically pleasing to most. However beautiful he was on the outside, laid no ground work for the stunning soul that poured out of him. Every word that oozed from his mouth was laced in suede and silk, and he beamed wit and understanding. Which is why when he heard the couple in front of him arguing vehemently, he thought he should get intervene: "Is there anything I can do to help you out," he inquired effortlessly. The man eyed Jacob with curiosity but it was almost obvious that curiosity veiled something deceitful. "Why don't you mind your own damn business college boy," the woman snarled. Jacob was taken aback, seeing as he had never been talked to that way in his life; he hid his shock and proceeded to try again, "You just seem like you could use some help ma'am, I didn't mean any offense. Do you need anything at all?" The woman sucked her teeth at Jacob and screeched at the man some more. Jacob tried once more, "If you need anything just let me know". Just as the last words left his mouth the man raised a hand gun to his temple and hissed, "You can shut the hell up and get on the floor". Jacob instantly tensed and felt his heart begin to quicken a pace. He stood frozen in his spot and vaguely heard the woman shouting, "Get on the ground now!" The man smiled a sleazy smile to Jacob that showed all of his blackened teeth and Jacob looked around him; everyone in the little shoppe was on the ground quivering with fear, and he was the only one besides the couple and the barista who was emptying the cash register standing. Jacob's eyes returned to the man's eyes which were gleaming with a devilish glow as he said evenly, "You've got three seconds college boy". Jacob shut his eyes tightly and gritted his teeth as he began lowering his body to tiled floor. Once he was down and the man turned his attention away from him, he began to carefully inch his hand toward his pocket to grab his cell phone. Just as he brushed the top and began sliding it out, he looked up and the woman was standing over him with her pistol aimed right between his eyes. Before he could blink the bullet was sailing through the air, and then through the soft skin of his forehead, and then through the thin layer of muscle beneath it, and then through the hard bone of his skull and into his pulsing brain. In those moments, as the tiny bullet pierced through each layer of his head, his thoughts flew to different moments of his life. Like the time his mother surprised him by baking dozens of cookies for his birthday and delivered them to his pee wee baseball practice. Or the first time he had ever kissed his girlfriend, Cindy, who he thought was the most iridescent creature that walked the earth. And even the time he had snuck out of his house at three in the morning just to ride his bike around the neighborhood. But the thought that his mind paused at and focused on as the bullet began to end his life, was when his father took him on a drive when he was seven years old down the pacific coast highway. Though he was too small to be in the front seat of his father's mustang, his dad had allowed him to anyway. He sat and looked out the window onto the seemingly endless ocean and listened as his father sang along with the radio. The song was by The Smith's, called "Asleep". His father's bass voice didn't match that of Morrissey at all but the words that chilled him as his father sang and that repeated in his head now were "*sing me to sleep, sing me to sleep, sing me to sleep*".

**About the Author:**

Alyssa Crowder is a nineteen year old Southern California native who is currently attending San Francisco State University. Alyssa is a Creative Writing major in sophomore standing at this current time.. Her focus is mainly fiction and poetry, with occasional tries at prose. She is inspired by many of her favorite bands such as The Smiths, The Fray, and Kings of Leon; her main novel of inspiration is *Crime and Punishment* by Fyodor Dostoevsky. Alyssa hopes to one day write the next Great American Novel. To read more of her writing, you can view her personal blog at *fictitiouswriter.tumblr.com*

# Indigenous Education
## John Tavares

A while ago in the town of Sioux Lookout, far from the bustling metropolis of Toronto, there once lived a boy who dreamt of escaping small town life and the poverty of the Indian reservation where he was born and raised. Akecheta wanted to become a doctor, but he occasionally considered that overambitious. Somehow, it became programmed in his mind—possibly, he was influenced by schoolteachers' speeches—he could succeed if he attended college and received an advanced education. So, when he graduated from high school, he applied for university in Toronto. He was told the bustling city was where his prospects for a promising career were best. Indeed, the university accepted him since his school grades were exceptional.

A problem he faced, though: he couldn't afford college. The modest amount he earned as a supermarket clerk was barely enough to pay for rent and food. So he was forced to apply to the provincial government for loans. Considered a First Nations person, though, the government expected him to apply for student grants from the reserve or obtain a loan from the federal department responsible for aboriginal affairs. Then, when he filled out the forms and photocopied documents, identification, and transcripts, and applied to the reserve, he found he wasn't accepted. His reserve band office expected him to live on their territory, to be eligible for a loan. They returned his application unprocessed, but added a cover letter, insisting in best bureaucratic style he query the federal department of education or Indian Affairs. Department officials promptly shot back a letter insisting his reserve had a program for improving access to postsecondary education for First Nations student, so he called the reserve band office. The reserve treasurer protested their funds were depleted, having met their annual quota for supporting postsecondary students and suggested applying to the province. Finally, provincial officials accepted his loan papers.

While working over the summer to pay debts incurred living alone during his high school years, he awaited word he'd qualify for loans so he could attend university in the fall. The time was filled with anxiety and excitement. He might finally get ahead in life and career, but realized that be impossible because he was young and Indian. Finally, he received word from the provincial postsecondary education loans officer, who wore a bow tie, a three-piece suit, and was slim and bald, that he qualified. He was eligible for a loan for tuition, and nothing else. They told him to obtain the living expenses from his reserve. Tsk-tsk. He remembered patience and understanding and not to become upset, as he was occasionally prone to fits and temper tantrums when, say, drinking with friends and buddies on a Saturday night in Sioux Lookout. He patiently filed the papers and, a few weeks later, a liaison officer from the federal government called him, mumbling he was calling on behalf of the education agency for his treaty region. Unfortunately, he didn't meet the legal criteria for consideration as an Indian eligible for educational grants since he didn't meet conditions as a reserve member eligible for postsecondary education grants. Akecheta sighed, saying he understood, but the bureaucracy bewildered him. Although sorely tempted to hang up, he patiently waited at the pay telephone in the foyer of the supermarket, where he had worked since he had started Queen Elizabeth District High School, until the government official murmured a curt, "That is all."

Meanwhile, he became concerned and anxious as daily he skipped coffee break in the upstairs lunchroom of the grocery store, walked to the post office, and checked his mailbox. But he only received mail from the provincial government and reserve demanding a notarized photocopy of his birth certificate, social insurance number card, provincial health number card, or a photocopy of his original certificate of Indian status or baptismal certificate. Several afternoons he changed a ten-dollar bill for coin with the cashier. While he stood outside the supermarket where he worked, in the foyer between the sliding doors, beside the shopping carts and bulletin board, he dialled call after call on the pay telephone, to the financial aid office for postsecondary student at the provincial government, to the department of postsecondary education for Indians at the federal government, to numerous officials and administrators to whom he was referred. When he finally connected with the proper officials, his was empty-handed. Then he called the band office, and asked them if he was still an Indian. They wearily replied, yes, he was still an Indian, but unentitled to financial aid. What kind of Indian did he think he was? If he expected grants or loans, he needed to live on reserve.

"But there are no jobs on the reserve," he protested.

"It doesn't matter. Those are the rules. We don't make them up."

Seeing no point in arguing, he wondered how he had stooped to disputing minutiae with bureaucrats and technocrats. He certainly wasn't ready to quit his job and move to the reserve to be eligible for grants, but that sounded like the prudent choice. Later, he took the train, moving to Toronto, before he was scheduled to enrol in university. He thought he might find a job, which would help pay for a place to stay. But because he was Indian and looked like an Indian, he thought, he wasn't hired anywhere. So, while he searched for a room and a job, he attended college, studying for his degree in chemistry. At night, he did his homework in the humanities library and, when the monolithic building closed late, he slept on the campus grounds. He placed his sleeping bag beneath a majestic maple tree beside a pond and studied for a while—until he had an encounter with a security guard. At four am while he boiled a kettle of water for instant coffee over a campfire, a security guard interrupted him. The guard gripped the canister of pepper spray in his utility belt. He asked to see his student identification. Then he was amazed when Aketchta provided the thick rigid plastic card.

"What are you doing here?"

"Sleeping."

"Well, I can see that. But what are you doing sleeping on campus?" He motioned across the pond towards the array of campus buildings besides the humanities complex. "Rez is over there."

"I tried the residences, but they said they ran out of space. Maybe they don't like Indians."

"It could be."

Akecheta was surprised he agreed with his supposition, but appreciated his plain-spokenness.

"And you're going to school here?"

Akecheta nodded. "I showed you my student card, didn't I?"

"It could be counterfeit."

"Seriously?" Akecheta examined his ID.

The security guard shrugged. "They make some of the best forged IDs on Yonge Street downtown."

"Yes, but campus isn't exactly downtown."

"Where are you from originally?"

"Thunder Trail Indian Reservation. But I lived in Sioux Lookout."

"Where's that?"

"In Northwestern Ontario."

"Where's that located?"

"It's near Thunder Bay."

Akecheta figured he might be talking to a Southern Ontario redneck or hick and didn't want to waste his time.

"Just forget it."

"You're crazy going to school here," the security guard said. "You know what this university is about? Making money from guys like you who should be working at a real job."

Akecheta thought, yes, this whole college enterprise seemed like a charade, the product of delusional ideation and crazy thinking. The guard ordered him off campus and wrote his student number from his photo identification card in his notepad. He warned him to leave or he'd summon the police and face charges of trespassing. When a backup security guard arrived, they escorted him off the grounds. Akecheta lingered near the bus stop and pretended to leave, but returned to collect his belongings. He left the campus in the middle of the night, moving his schoolbooks and personal belongings in a backpack and duffle bag. He managed to persuade the driver of the night bus to allow him to ride to the stop furthest south where he took a transfer and rode along Bloor Street until he reached a park beside the Don Valley and Bloor Street Viaduct where he decided to stay the night. Undisturbed, he stayed in the park and found shelter at the edge of the forest located near the Don Valley parkway. He did his homework with a flashlight and from the lamps of the Bloor Street Viaduct, which spanned high above the Don Valley. Then he climbed the embankment, sleeping in the grass near the embankments.

He commuted to the university campus each morning, earning enough for fare each month by collecting recyclable beer cans and liquor bottles discarded throughout the park. The trip took over ninety minutes during rush hour traffic, during which he read his textbooks and did homework. After the run-in with the security guard, when he returned to campus, he discovered that he was followed, but refrained from protesting his annoyance and harassment at security guards trailing him everywhere. He visited the front desk of the residence and explained his situation to the residential director, but she said she could nothing for him. They might have a room for him, but he didn't meet requirements. What requirements? She wouldn't say. He was dark and dirty was all she could think, as she pinched her face. And he had the facial profile—the rugged chin and chiseled cheeks of fierce, proud warriors she observed on Western movies she watched late at night on CBC television years ago. Wanting him to vacate the premises, she commanded he leave the front desk immediately. She called security and two guards in body armour escorted him from the residence building as he left of his own volition. As he walked out the door, frustrated, carrying a backpack of books, the door slammed.

Soon Akecheta settled into a routine. He brought homework to a café or restaurant downtown and worked on his studies while he sipped coffee and ate a muffin. He managed to score at the top of his class in most courses, but the schoolwork proved a trial. He continued to live alongside the parkway and the sluggish river that snaked beneath the Bloor Street Viaduct, napping in a sleeping bag in warm clothes, collecting recyclables, beer cans and liquor bottles, which occasionally earned him a surprising amount of cash.

Several times, as he read a textbook or took notes from his squat near the bluff that overlooked the valley and the parkway, he witnessed a spectacle that remained indelible in memory. He saw the silhouettes of figures walk along the walkway on the Bloor Street Viaduct and, while cars, trucks, motorcycles, and bicycles whizzed by, they climbed the guardrail of the bridge. Some paced restlessly and then leapt. Some crossed themselves and then fell. Others gesticulated, shouted and then climbed over the guardrail. Some sobbed, cried, and then plunged. Some simply dropped from the steel guardrail of the bridge as if they were placing the weekly garbage on the curb. They plummeted for several seconds, usually head down until they crashed to the highway, trail, or parkway below, their bodies crushed. Each time he climbed the path to the pay telephone located beside the bridge, called 911, and informed the emergency dispatcher. Then he hung up the phone, hoping there was a prospect the jumpers might still be alive, although frankly he doubted they could survive such a fall. The first few suicide attempts he witnessed he tried to help and continued chest compressions until the ambulance arrived. After the ambulance finally arrived, a paramedic strode up. As he hovered over the prostate form of a woman, the paramedic said he was an idiot. He fractured a rib on a man the last time he tried to save somebody. Now he feared becoming involved. One night he climbed the guardrail and glanced down from the fearsome height, thinking he should jump. In the end, he changed his mind, thinking of the wasted effort, coming to Toronto from Sioux Lookout to be a student. He simply didn't want to surrender so soon and perish from a fall from the Bloor Street Viaduct high above the Don Valley.

Still, he found life as a student living in the park beside the Bloor Street Viaduct and the Don Valley Parkway more than a challenge. When he managed to escape the park near the valley and tried to work on his homework in the public library or the university library, he found that he was harassed by security guards and students believing they were security guards, people believing he was dealing drugs or that he was homeless, looking for a place to hang out or nap. Well, he was homeless, but he was working on his school assignments in the ties library. Then, when he hiked downtown to work on his schoolwork in a café he found himself harassed by undercover officers. The narcs in the coffee shops wanted him involved in drugs deals. But he didn't consume illicit drugs, and was reluctant to take prescription medications. He had no drugs to sell, and they were wasting everybody's time.

Finally, after a tutorial assistant argued with him, and threatened to fail him, Akecheta managed to finish the term with enough credits for a university degree. By accident, he met a professor as he left the library late one night. Having been drinking at the faculty lounge, as was her want whenever she had an article published in a distinguished academic journal, the professor pressed close. Upbeat, she insisted he attend the graduation ceremony. Heartened by her smile and prettiness, he decided to attend the convocation as her date. When he was called to the stage of the college auditorium, he received the diploma from a man he thought looked familiar, the former premier of the province, he guessed, recalling the newspapers he read during coffee break. Indeed, it was the former premier, but the natural born pol, silver-haired, dressed in the finest suit Akecheta had ever seen, looked dismayed. Appearing as if he was suffering a severe case of constipation, the distinguished politician and university chancellor apparently thought ill of Akecheta. As he accepted his degree, the professor thought the former premier was leering at him. ("He was," the professor muttered repeatedly afterwards.) Akecheta beamed and walked away with his scrolled degree. He unfurrowed it and studied the paper with bemusement and puzzlement. He wondered what the past few stressful years had been about—the work and effort for this piece of paper. He continued to contemplate this fact, as months afterwards, with his degree, he still couldn't find a job. He eventually loaded his backpack and, in the rail yards, simply boarded an empty boxcar on the next freight train back to his hometown of Sioux Lookout.

**About the Author:**
Born and raised in Sioux Lookout, Ontario, John is the son of Portuguese immigrants from the Azores. He is a graduate of the arts and science program at Humber College, journalism at Centennial College, and recently earned an Honours BA Specialized in English at York University in Toronto. His short fiction has appeared in literary magazines such as Blood & Aphorisms, Filling Station, Tessera, Windsor Review, and Gertrude as well as online publications such as The Write Place at the Write Time, The Writing Disorder, and The Maple Tree Literary Supplement. His journalism has appeared in several Toronto community newspapers and trade publications such as Hospital News, and he has volunteered as a community radio broadcaster with CBLS-CBQW in Sioux Lookout.

# FLASH FICTION

# The Locked Out
## Daniel Perry

There were two locks: bolt and latch. From the street he turned his key, clunking the bolt, but when he pulled the door it didn't open. It was nine o'clock, Saturday morning, and his love slept heavily inside the apartment above the shop. Her shift at the hospital had ended at four a.m., while he, finished work for the week, was asleep at a friend's house after drinking beer until the wee hours. It had begun raining around midnight and as neither he nor the friend owned an umbrella, he'd chosen the couch instead of walking home, texting her saying he would return in the morning. When she had entered, tired and presumably drenched, she must have thought nothing of sliding the latch across.

A call would wake her most gently, so he dialled from his Blackberry, but her voicemail answered before any rings - her phone was off, or silenced. He texted and then he sent a short email, hoping one or the other would trigger a different sound. When neither received a response he sipped coffee from his paper cup and frowned. The rain was still falling, and overnight the wind had picked up. His wet T-shirt clung to him and his feet squished in his sneakers' decaying soles.

Knocking would make next to no noise, as the door was a metal framed piece of oft-graffitied frosted glass. Tapping it with a key or a coin was louder, and he tried it but still she didn't come down the stairs. The push-button buzzer never had worked, and when he needed in his habit was to pull and push the handle rapidly so that the door banged on the jamb. But the thundering would be hell to awake to, especially after working so late. He heard a click and looked down to where the cat's silhouette inside put two clawed paws on the glass and stretched before it lay down. *A dog would bark*, he thought. He exhaled and gripped the handle and banged banged banged and waited. Nothing. He looked down at the animal's vague outline and tried to commune with it: *Go get her,* he willed and then said, lowering himself into a squat before the door, which drew a strange look from the shop owner who had come to investigate. *You can sit in my store,* he said, but the locked out declined, saying, *She'll just be a minute. I'll try again.* The shop owner smiled and returned to his counter, his door chime jingling behind him.

On the wet street a car hissed as it passed, masking the locked out's exhalation as he shook the door, trying to make enough noise without sounding desperate, or violent, or drunk - which he wasn't, and hadn't been the night before. But maybe he should have gotten soaked in the dark, the way she must have during her walk home. Maybe when he texted to say he was staying out he dashed her dream of peeling off their wet clothes with teeth chattering and stepping into a hot shower, up too late but being so together and then crawling into bed like they had in university after too-loud music and shawarma when the bars closed. Maybe she had latched the door on purpose.

He began walking down the street, composing another text: *At the library, call me when you wake up.* From the shelf he chose a dog-eared copy of *The Lottery* and he sat at a central table reading its first story, "The Intoxicated." He looked repeatedly at the Blackberry, set to silent, and he waited for its little red light to blink.

He wondered when the rain would stop.

**About the Author:**

Daniel Perry's stories have been shortlisted for the Carter V. Cooper Short Fiction Prize and have been published in more than 20 Canadian print and online magazines, including *The Dalhousie Review*, *Exile Literary Quarterly*, *Maple Tree Literary Supplement*, and *Little Fiction*, as well as the Stone Skin Press anthology *The Lion and the Aardvark*. He lives in Toronto, and on Twitter @danielperrysays.

# Story
## HC Hsu

He wasn't sure exactly how it happened, but he ended up cumming inside her.

She said: Tell me.

He remembered. It began with a story.

He continued:

'And I ran into an old cleaning guy, an old Asian man, who looked like my father. It was after school, so custodians were cleaning the restrooms. He was sweeping and didn't look up at me, so I went into the restroom and waited for like an hour. No one came, so I jerked off and shot my load on the toilet.'

'Another time, this guy stuck his hand under the stall motioning me to slide my dick under. Right then the restroom door flung open, and a little girl ran in, shouting "Papi! Papi!" and ducking her head under all the stall doors to check for her father. Before she got to mine the man next to me started shouting something in Spanish. I could see the shadow of his hands moving on the tiles. After the little girl ran out and left he tapped his foot again, got up and slid his bare legs and cock, about eight inches, brown, foreskin pulled back, glistening at the tip, under the partition. I pulled up my pants and left instead. As I was walking out, I ran into a Mexican woman standing right outside the bathroom door, staring daggers into me. I quickly left, but didn't see the little girl anywhere.'

He finally pulled out, rolling onto his back, on the bed.

Is this another one of your made-up stories about your father? She smiled, rolling her eyes at him.

(Ha ha, yeah. Sorry.)

*Another father-copy. Another prox*

She: Where is your story going, anyway?

He: I don't know.

(Keywords: origins, genealogy, pedigree.)

*Who is really your father? The interrogator struck his face and held up the light between his eyes.*

*

She said: 'It's ok. I'm on the pill.'

**About the Author:**
HC Hsu was born in Taipei. He is the author of the short story collection *Love Is Sweeter* (Lethe, May 2013). Finalist for the 2013 Wendell Mayo Award and *The Austin Chronicle* 21st Short Story Prize, First Place Winner of A Midsummer Tale 2013, Third Prize Winner of the 2013 *Memoir* essay competition, and *The Best American Essays 2014* Nominee, he has written for *Words Without Borders*, *Two Lines*, *PRISM International*, *Renditions*, *Far Enough East*, and many others. He has served as translator for the US Congressional-Executive Commission on China and is currently a research fellow at the Europäische Universität für Interdisziplinäre Studien, Switzerland, where he is completing a commissioned translation of 2010 Nobel Peace Prize recipient Liu Xiaobo's biography.

## She's Perfect
## Joseph Edscorn

I'm nervous, why am I nervous? I shouldn't be nervous. This day has been coming for a while! It's not news for me or anything. Yet here I am, with my heart racing and my foot tapping a hole into the ground.

The music starts and everyone stands. I'm already standing, I'm standing next to the altar, dressed in my custom ordered tux. Everyone's dressed up for the special day. I don't know why my heart's beating so fast. Well I guess I do. I put my best smile on and watch as she comes through the chapel doors.

My best friend, still as beautiful as ever. She's the love of my life and I would literally do anything for her. I've been there for her since day one and she did the same for me. I remember when she got hit by the car and I sat by her bedside for three days straight until she woke up.

When I had my surgery she sat by my bedside in return. We travelled the world together and experienced so many things together.

She's been my first and only love. I love her smile that shines brighter than the sun. I love her dark brown hair that flows around her face like a halo. I love her eyes, brown as melted chocolate. I love the way she laughs and how she walks.

Speaking of walking, she's half way up the aisle now. My heart won't stop racing, the music tempo couldn't keep up if the pianist had ten hands. I stare at her and she smiles that wonderful smile. She reaches the altar and the words start rolling on and on. I couldn't hear them. They're all a blur to me as I look at her perfect face.

When I hear her name, the whole world slows around me and my heart speeds up. My stomach gets light and my mind goes off into another world of happiness. She's like a drug to me, a drug that I could never quit even if I wanted to. Not that I ever would. I've been following her around for as long as I could remember.

When we were kids I would latch on to her hand and she would drag me with her everywhere. I didn't know how to be anything without her.

As she says those two little words, all I can think is that she's perfect in every way except for one thing; she's getting married today and I'm the best man.

**About the Author:**

Joseph Edscorn started writing before he could really understand the meaning of "plot." He grew up in Jaffrey, New Hampshire with his family of seven and his dog Stormy, who became the inspiration for his first work of writing- a piece that remains unfinished. This piece is Joseph's first professional attempt at realism; really his heart belongs to science fiction. If you want to see more of Joseph's writing you can like him on facebook.

# FEATURED POET

CARL MILLER DANIELS lives in the United States. He's not a cowboy, but thinks about them a lot. His poems have appeared in many nice places, including Chiron Review, Citizens for Decent Literature, The Commonline Journal, FUCK!, My Favorite Bullet, and Zygote in my Coffee. Daniels has three chapbooks in print. And his first full-length book, Gorilla Architecture, was recently published by Interior Noise Press. His next full-length book, Saline, is in the works, also at Interior Noise Press. Daniels and his partner, Jon (aka "the sweetest man in the world"), have lived together for over 30 years.

## the british are coming
## Carl Miller Daniels

calling out the guard to protect my misspent youth
is like getting a fly swatter to kill a mountain lion.
calling out a sexy naked big-dicked teenage boy
to protect my misspent old age is like
commanding everyone, everywhere, to
cease masturbating, once and for all.
people keep expecting logic and
reasonable transitions from Point A to
Point B. people have all kinds of
expectations. hopes and dreams,
vaulted hypotheses of the ease of
testing what is right and what is
wrong, and sensing the earnest value of
good movies when coupled with
too much wine. i tell you,
when that sexy naked big-dicked teenage boy
is lying on his back on top of his bed
at midnight, and his big throbbing dick
is hard as a rock, and he's trying to
follow the rules against masturbation,
and he's looking at himself
in the mirror that's mounted over his
dresser-top, but which conveniently
shows his entire beautiful slim tawny naked
body within the confines of its
metallic frame, it's difficult for this
sexy naked big-dicked teenage boy
to keep his fingers off his
big throbbing dick, and
he smiles into the mirror,
as he waits for his erection
to subside, on its own, and
thereby relieve him of decisions,
and acts of retrogression, as
he slithers succinctly into
that state of mind where

peacocks stand in the treetops
and scream their heads off,
their big feathers fluffed up
and spread out, all
shiny in the noon-day sun

# golden age penis skeleton
## Carl Miller Daniels

the sexy naked big-dicked teenage boy had reached
the point in his masturbatory development where
he liked to whap his dick against his belly.
in other words, he liked to lie on his back atop
his bed,
and with the fingers of one hand hold onto
his dick so
that he could knock the top of his dick
against his belly, rhythmically, whap
whap whap.
the sexy naked big-dicked teenage boy
especially savored the feel of his
big purple dickhead as he knocked
the top of it against his smooth
tight belly. whap whap whap.
oh yes,
the sexy naked big-dicked teenage boy
loved to lie there atop his bed on his
back whapping the top of his big hard
dick against his nice smooth and tight
belly. this procedure made a definite
"whap whap whap" sound and one
night he was lying in bed masturbating
using that method and
making that "whap whap whap" sound
as the top of his big hard dick whapped
against his belly,
and his roommate said "what
are you doing?"
his roommate was also a sophomore
in college. his roommate was in
the top bunk.
he himself was in the bottom bunk.
his roommate was also a very good-looking
guy.
so, the mood he was in,

the sexy naked big-dicked teenage boy
who was currently masturbating
and making that "whap whap whap" sound
said: "i'm doing this new kind of
masturbation i've starting liking where
i whap the top of my dick against my belly.
it feels great, especially the part where my
my nice sensitive dickhead whaps against
me."
and, while saying these words to
his sexy roommate,
the sexy naked big-dicked teenage boy
is making that "whap whap whap" sound
as he continues masturbating using this
"whap whap whap" methodology.
in a couple of seconds, the sexy roommate
replies, "that's what i thought you
were doing," and then HE, the sexy roommate,
begins making that sound himself, as he
whaps the top of his own big smooth dick
against his own nice taut belly.
so both boys are lying in their bunks,
masturbating in this "whap whap whap"
method, neither boy seeing
the other, but both boys entirely aware
of what is going on, and very soon,
they are pacing themselves using
the exact same rhythm. their
"whap whap whaps" are synchronized
exactly, and then both sophomore college boys,
the sexy naked big-dicked teenage boy
and his hot sexy roommate,
are chuckling good-naturedly,
lying there masturbating rhythmically,
and the sexy naked big-dicked teenage boy
says to his roommate,
"any second i'm gonna spurt cum" and
his sexy roommate answers back "me too"
and
the "whap whap whap" continues right along,
until a moment of silence,

during which hot smelly cum is being spurted
in great big gooey gushy quantities.
then, both boys get out of bed
and start wiping the cum off
their chests and bellies with
dirty t-shirts,
and
the lights in their room are still
off
but
suddenly
the sexy naked big-dicked teenage boy
turns on the overhead light
and both boys stand there
staring at each other,
their big dicks still mostly
hard, their bodies young
and beautiful and sweaty,
they've never done anything like
this before, nothing sexual like
this, with each other, or with
any other guy for that matter,
and
they just go on staring at each
other like this is the most
amazing thing they've ever done
in their whole entire
lives
and, years later,
all graduated,
employed, with attractive
wives and smart sassy kids,
each of those two guys
occasionally thinks back
on that night in the dorm,
and then each of those
two guys grins, licks
his lips, and
smiles really really
big.

## taking credit for sunday
## Carl Miller Daniels

monsters rise up out of the ocean and attack
the land. then, as if thinking they have done
something good, they wait to be patted
on the head by sexy naked big-dicked teenage boys.
then, in addition, they roll onto their sides
and offer their assholes to be fucked
by the sexy naked big-dicked teenage boys who
now have full raging hardons. what
sexy naked big-dicked teenage boy, and in
that state of arousal, could resist
that kind of offer? and so,
the sexy naked big-dicked teenage boys
pat the monsters on the head
and fuck them up the ass. then,
they roll apart, these freshly-fucked
head-patted monsters and
the sexy naked big-dicked teenage boys
who have just head-patted them and butt-fucked them,
and the monsters slink back into
the sea, once again, thinking they have done
something good. then the sexy naked big-dicked
teenage boys lie there alone on the sand,
staring up at the sky, worshipping faith and
hope, and craving the meaning of charity.
when the time arrives
for the sexy naked big-dicked teenage boys
to spurt another load of
cum, the
warning sirens go off and everyone
starts milling about. there is
high anxiety on the beach. nothing
seems certain. and it is
only the very lucky, who
bend over, wait, and
grab ahold of
their own ankles, as

the sexy naked big-dicked teenage boys
roam about, making difficult,
though well-reasoned, choices.

## kangaroo vine gold rush
## Carl Miller Daniels

ralph the nation and pantomime the stars,
the manikins are coming to town. and why is
it, you may ask, that manikins have no
genitalia? males or females, the
manikins just don't have these organs.
the sexy big-dicked teenage boys are standing
in front of a window display, where
all the manikins are still nude, and
are just this moment being dressed, and
it is hard not to notice that
none of these manikins have
genitalia. "where are the guys' dicks?" says
one of the sexy big-dicked teenage boys.
"and where are the girls' cunts?" says
another of the sexy big-dicked teenage boys.
then, the sexy big-dicked teenage boys
stand there a while longer, until
the manikins are mostly dressed,
and then,
nearing sunset,
the sexy big-dicked teenage boys
head on over to the house
where one of them lives,
and they take off all their
clothes, and they look at
each other's genitals. and by
look, i mean really look.
these sexy naked big-dicked teenage boys
examine each other's genitals,
scrutinize each other's genitals,
talk about each other's genitals,
and, the general consensus is,
that everybody here looks real good naked,
and that everybody here has real nice
genitals, and that boy manikins everywhere
should definitely have genitals, too.

by then, all the sexy naked big-dicked
teenage boys have pretty much
fallen in love with each other,
and they touch each other
in warm, friendly, and
overtly sexual ways. in fact, when
the word "orgy" is spoken,
there is instant agreement,
and
even the sexy male manikin that's
been hidden in the
mother's closet, gets to
take part. none of the
boys are surprised to see
that this particular manikin
has a penis,
or that his
eyes are startlingly
blue.

## the evolutionary squawk
## Carl Miller Daniels

"ambrosia for the masses,
but only turnips for the elite?"
thinks the sexy naked big-dicked teenage boy.
"that doesn't seem fair, now does it?"
**
the sexy naked big-dicked teenage boy
is bothered by a sense
of fairness, by a sense of what
is, and is not, fair play in
the day-to-day operations of the world.
**
"and why should the masses
be the main market for
all the big beautiful blockbuster movies, and,
for us, the elite, there's just
these scrawny little indie films?"
**
oh yes, the sexy naked big-dicked teenage boy
knows quite well that his own
status is firmly with the elite,
and that he, and the masses,
have never traveled the same path.
**
the sexy naked big-dicked teenage boy
is a worrier, too, as he
stands there in
a secluded spot in the forest,
staring up into the sky, as
if searching for answers.
**
the sexy naked big-dicked teenage boy
is tugging on his own big
sweet beautiful dick,
now hard as a rock,
as the birds sing, and the
butterflies flutter about.

there's a droplet of perfectly
clear, and sticky, pre-cum at
the tip of his dick, and
he's just about at the moment
of orgasm.
**
"this business of equality,"
thinks the sexy naked big-dicked teenage boy,
as he tugs on his own big
beautiful dick, "when
clearly i'm good-looking and gifted
and sexy as hell, is certainly
a matter for further contemplation,"
thinks the sexy naked big-dicked teenage boy,
as the moment of orgasm
arrives, his cum begins to
spurt, and his tight little
nipples tingle like bright
copper pennies, hitting the
pavement, as the traffic
slows to a stop.

**Mission Statement:**
One of my favorite quotes, and I'm going to approximate it/paraphrase it here, because I'm waaaaaaay too lazy to actually look it up anywhere, is by some writer who said that he writes out of an infantile need for attention. He said, for him, writing was akin to stamping his feet and demanding to be noticed. Sheesh. I don't know if that's true of me. But I do write because it's fun. Honest to gosh, it's fun. And, it helps pass the time! There's a quote I like, and it's only tangentially related to your question, but I'll quote it here now anyway, and I do know the source of this one. Here's the quote: "Poetry and drink are the two greatest things on earth." ~ Richard Burton, Actor.

## About Writers:

Writers trying to break bounds fail. Writers being true to their aim achieve that end. No one should try to change the world. They just one day do.

~ Damon Ferrell Marbut

www.ingramcontent.com/pod-product-compliance
Lightning Source LLC
LaVergne TN
LVHW011052110826
845149LV00015B/3472

* 9 7 8 0 9 9 2 0 3 5 5 3 2 *